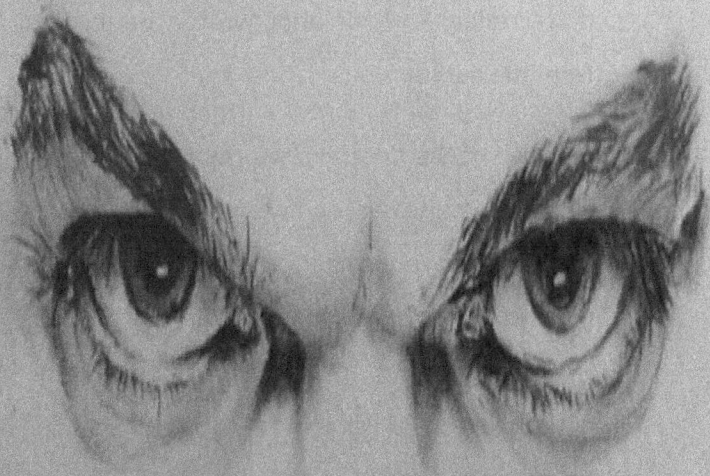

Disclaimer

Contents

Foreword

With an extensive increase in the rate of crime all over the world and especially in America, the need to address the underlying causes responsible for this alarming rise has never been more urgent. Since murder stands at the apex of the crime hierarchy, this book focuses on one of the vilest crimes that the hands of humankind are capable of committing. It deals with the serious and ever increasing phenomenon of serial killing.

This manuscript is based on the detailed research carried out by Darren Freeman, a Former Law Enforcement Administrative Commander and Criminal Law Instructor, and his several years of practical experience with serial killers. His research paper "Profiling the serial killer" tackles the societal nuisance brought forth by homicidal maniacs with profound analytics and accuracy and deals majorly with identifying a serial killer. This book, however, is crafted to take a deeper look at the scenario by further investing in exploring the behaviors as well as the sociological and psychological factors affecting the minds and actions of these affected individuals.

It starts off with a detailed history of murders and gradually progresses to the topics of serial killers, their types, their motivations, and their methods. Moreover, it takes a look at the lives of famous serial killers considering them as model samples for observations sake. It further investigates the role of gender in determining the nature and chances of the crime. Finally, it looks at facts and figures to establish ways in which such a crime can be prevented.

Chapter 1

Jack the Ripper

Murder is not a modern phenomenon and is definitely not an entirely American concept. The act of killing another person without the interference of law has been a constant occurrence around the world. Historians claim that our society has been witnessing it as early as the1600's. The origins of murder lie in Ancient Rome and have moved forward through the centuries.

Similarly, there have been chronicles of serial killers in the ancient times as well. European Dr. Richard von Krafft-Ebing conducted the first documented research in the 19th century. It dealt with the violent felonies of sexual offenders, focusing mainly on their crimes of sexual proclivity, homicide, and serial murders.

The details can be found in his most famous book, Psychopathia Sexualis.

However, serial murder is a relatively less common phenomenon and makes just one percent of the murders committed in a year. Yet, the horrors of the crime and the haunting macabre that surrounds the topic of serial killing are interesting to many minds. Therefore, it has inspired a number of fiction and non-fiction literature, not to mention the various movies that have drawn over the idea to top the charts.

This incessant public obsession over this gruesome acts of Violence began in the last part of the year 1880 when a series of unsolved murders were uncovered around the White Chapel area in London. This was the first case of its kind to get unearthed and is termed as the pioneer act of a huge phenomenon that later took the shape of serial killings. The unidentified diseased mind behind the crime called himself Jack the Ripper, mutilated and killed 5 prostitutes, and continued to confess his crimes via letters sent straight to the Police.

Here is an excerpt from one of his shockingly horrible letters:

I am down on whores and I shant quit ripping them till I do get buckled. Grand work the last job was. I gave the lady no time to squeal. How can they catch me now. I love my work and want to start again. You will soon hear of me with my funny little games.

His letters portrayed that the words were coming from a diseased mind. For example:

The next job I do I shall clip the lady's ears off and send to the police officers just for jolly wouldn't you.

My knife is so nice and sharp I want to get to work right away if I get a chance. Good luck.

He would then sign his letter as:

Yours truly
Jack the Ripper

Since this was the first case of serial killing, this *nom de guerre* of Jack the Ripper and these murders are now used as synonyms of serial murder. This strange case of murders has spawned a number of legends about serial murders as well as real serial killers

Later, the murder cases of similar nature were witnessed during the 1970's and 80's. The most famous serial killers that sprang from this time period seemed to be hugely impressed and inspired by Jack the Ripper. These include Ted Bundy, Green River Killer, and BTK. These murderers sparked the public interest, which was further fueled by the release of movies concerning the topics of serial killing in the 1990s, of which Silence of the Lambs is a classic example.

While many like to believe that serial killing is either a part of the past or a topic only suitable for movies and books, this is not the case. The trend has somehow seeped into the modern society as well. According to the Crime statistics on serial killing, 35 to 50 active serial killers are estimated to be present across America at a particular time period. The threat of serial killing in the United States of America has never been nearer.

Chapter 2

Serial Killers and their Types

In earlier times, when comprehensive knowledge on the murders and their types was not available due to lack of sufficient research on the topic, legal authorities had classified them all under the single category of homicide. This created a general disregard for the different types of murders and the motivations behind it. As a result, it was impossible to devise a scientific way to study and identify the thought pattern and actions of a criminal.

Soon, the need to study different methods of killing was evaluated in detail, which helped the law enforcement in recognizing various types of homicides. Consequently, the extensive studies conducted in this regard identified three separate types of murder.

Types of Murder

A homicide is divided into the following three types:

- **Mass Murder**

This is defined as a onetime eruption of brutality that happens at a single location and affects a number of people. According to the criterion defined by FBI, there should be at least 4 victims for a killing to be classified as a mass murder.

- **Spree Killing**

In this case, the murderer kills a string of individuals at varying locations but with the absence of a cooling off period between the killings.

- **Serial Killing**

An episode of murders where there are several murders at different locations over a time span and a cooling off period is present too.

Serial killings have been identified under different names throughout history as well. For example, Cormier in 1972 coined the term 'multicide' for defining various murders committed by a single person but over an elaborate time period. Similarly, in the 1800's, the Germans had been reported to use the word "lustmord" for such killings, which translates in English to 'murder for pleasure.'

The first most comprehensive definition of serial murder came in the year 1983 by Egger. According to this definition, serial killings comprise of more than one murder committed by a single or a number of individuals where the victims are strangers for the murderers and the acts are carried out at different geographical localities.

Moreover, Egger emphasized that the motive behind the murders in serial killings has nothing to do with material gain and it is more of a compulsive act performed specifically to gratify the murderer. Moreover, Egger drafted that the victims of serial killings often belong to the lower and powerless socio-economic groups.

In the year 1984, Douglas, D' Agostino, Burgess, and Ressler provided a new definition of serial murders. Their definition was essentially similar to the one given by Egger but they specified the time period between the killings to range from 2 days to weeks or months. They termed this time period as the cooling off period.

Holmes and DeBurger provided another popular definition of serial killings in the year1988. They wrote in their famous manuscript, "Serial Murder" that a serial killing is characterized by the presence of certain elements. These elements throw light on the specific traits that are portrayed by a serial murderer. These traits include the following:

- They repeat the homicides and continue unless prevented
- The victim-perpetrator relationship does not exist. They are either complete strangers or only slightly acquainted
- The motivation behind the killing is in most cases not a conventional one. It is neither victim precipitated nor has any material motive behind it
- There is never an intrinsic motive behind these serial killings

Serial killings have been studied in detail as attempts have been made to dig deeper into the psychology and behavior of individuals who are drawn to perform such heinous activities without any remorse. Finding this information is not only crucial in identifying people with such revolting tendencies but also to learn the reasons behind such behaviors.

As a result of detailed studies, psychologists and researchers have succeeded in classifying the serial killers into different categories. This will be helpful in understanding how the brains of such individuals work and what are the reasons behind their behavior.

Types of Serial Killers

Owing to the studies conducted by Dr. Holmes and Dr. DeBurger in 1988, there are four different types of serial killers. These are discussed below in detail:

- **Visionary Serial Killers**

Visionary serial killers are the ones that claim to hear voices in their heads that tell them to do the killings or they have visions of a similar nature. They are said to suffer from one or another form of psychosis. Their victims are not specifically targeted and they are said to function under hallucinations and delusions.

Example of this type of killer is the famous Indonesian killer Ahmad Suradji. He was an ordinary cattle breeder but then he dreamt of his dead father directing him to kill 70 women and drink their saliva. Believing it to be a divine intervention that will build his spiritual powers, he carried forward the plan. However, he was caught after murdering his 42nd victim and did not reach his mark of 70 women.

- **Mission oriented Serial Killers**

According to Dr. Ronald Holmes' book, "The World of Serial Killers", this is the second type of serial killer. Their motive behind committing the murders is to rid the world of evil and cleansing it by killing the individuals that are undesirable. They work with a goal and target people with particular traits.

There are various examples of mission-oriented serial killers and most of their targets had been women such as prostitutes, people belonging to a particular ethnicity or religion, and homosexuals. This type of serial killing comes quite close to hate crime.

Joseph Paul Franklin, an American serial killer of the 1970s is a model example of a mission-oriented serial killer. He was found guilty of depriving 12 black males of their lives. He claimed to kill them because they had white girl friends. Surprisingly, despite the severity of his crimes, William Luther Pierce, a white supremacist, ennobled him by writing a fictional novel by the title, "Hunter", which was inspired by Joseph and his crimes.

- **Hedonistic Serial Killers**

The third type of murderers are driven by thrill, lust, and comfort. Their sole purpose is to seek pleasure, which they somehow get from killing off people. Basically, they just kill for the kicks.

Tyler Hadley killed his parents just to have a party at this house. He invited the whole town and hid the bodies of his dead parents in their bedroom. Nobody suspected anything and loved the party until he confessed his crime to his childhood friend. When his friend refused to believe him, he showed him the dead bodies.

- **Power or Control Oriented Serial Killer**

This is the last major type of serial killers. Serial murderers belonging to this category kill for the purpose of seeking control and dominance. They find it satisfying that the life of another individual is completely at their mercy. Some of the hedonistic serial killers are mainly driven by sex too.

Jane Toppan is a classic example of a control-oriented serial killer. She had a disturbing childhood and later grew to become a nurse. While all her patients adored her, they all ended up dead. When she was caught, she admitted to killing 33 individuals. Her love for power and control was evident from her method of killing. She tortured her victims between life and death by injecting morphine that brought them close to death and then reviving them with a dose of atropine.

What really startled the public was her defense plea where she claimed to murder so many people because she did not have a family of her own to divert her attention.

Classifying the serial killers under relevant categories has an academic advantage and allows the researchers to study specific cases in detail. As such, several theories are identified that can explain the psychology of a particular type of serial killer but only to some extent. Further research needs to be done to perfect the field. For now, it is almost impossible to 'catch' a serial killer but once caught; you can definitely analyze them with the current knowledge.

Therefore, the next section in this book sheds light on what the motivations are behind a particular serial killer's need to kill.

Chapter 3

Motivations behind the need to kill

Many people argue that contrary to the popular belief, a majority of the serial killers are not crazy. In fact, a great many of them are reported to have extremely distinguished careers in their fields. Yet, this does not rule out the possibility of a hidden psychosis either. There are several reports where these individuals have been reported to have hallucinations directing them to commit specific acts of felony.

The classic definition of a serial murder, provided by Levin and Fox in the year 1985 in their book, "Mass Murder" describes the pathology of a serial killer's mind. It states that, *"A serial killer travels around even from one state to another in some cases, searches for particular type of victims to rape, dismember, torture, stab, and strangle"*.

While this definition portrays the sadistic behavior of these individuals, it still tells us that they are more evil than they are crazy. The serial killers who are driven by hallucinations and delusions make a very small percentage of the total occurrences of serial killings. Moreover, there are no instances of talking to demons and a lot of these claims are nothing but the attempts made by these people to escape punishment.

The supporters of the theory that serial killers are not crazy claim that such individuals have a sickening mindset but they are not legally or medically sick. Such individuals have more of a sociopath personality where they lack integrity, control, or conscience to direct their behavior. On the contrary, they have a strong need of controlling and dominating other people. They might have addictive urges to do what they do but they know right from wrong. When they commit an act of immorality, they know perfectly well that they have acted in an immoral manner. Yet, they simply do not care about other humans and their pain.

Researchers have made attempts to identify the motivation that drives an individual to commit a tremendously indecent act of villainy. The most popular theory explaining a serial killer's need to kill is their antisocial personality. A person suffering from such a condition displays the following characteristics:

- Intelligence
- Superficial charm
- Poor judgment
- Failure to learn from the past mistakes
- Untruthful, unreliable, and insincere
- Egocentric to the point of being pathogenic

- Incapacity to love
- Lack of nervousness

According to various researchers, this kind of behavior is common among sociopaths and a great number of serial killers portray this behavior as well. Serial killers engage in criminal acts as they experience tension and anxiety. However, their gruesome behavior causes them no harm as they are free of guilt and remorse.

According to Sears, a deficiency in the psychological makeup of a person may cause them to act in a sickening manner as their normal emotional development is hindered. Another researcher, Quay, has stated that a serial murderer could be a psychopathic hybrid. This theory could explain their greater need of finding stimuli. Moreover, it could also account for their need to kill repeatedly.

Serial Killers' Need to Kill

Several studies have been conducted to identify the motive behind murders. While there could be a number of reasons behind a murder, they can be classified under two broad groups. These include:

- Murders driven by an altercation, such as a quarrel, as an answer to an insult, jealousy, fit/rage
- Murders committed for gaining a benefit such as self protection, monetary gains, or power

Two famous researchers, Holmes and DeBurger in 1988, defined these groups. While the two definitions are ideal for explaining most of the murders, most of the serial killings fail to fall under the two categories. For serial killers, power and money are almost never the reasons of their brutality and only a minute percentage of the serial killers came under the first category.

In fact, most of them just kill for the sake of killing. Even when they are not gaining anything from the murders, they derive pleasure and satisfaction from the act. Many psychologists and researchers who have studied these individuals for years have concluded that serial killers' need to kill is similar to our need to drink water. Just as one glass is not enough for us to last a day, one murder is not sufficient to cure them of their sick mindset. They will keep needing more and more of it.

When it comes to serial killings in particular, the authors Holmes and DeBurger, did a detailed research in order to find out about the behavior patterns and background of the serial killers. Their aim was to discover about the motivation that drives these individuals, as they are clearly not about revenge or personal gains.

They explored the topic by focusing on the following four major aspects:

- The past of the perpetrator
- The victim's characteristics
- Method and pattern of killing
- Location of the murders

Moreover, the criminal's behavior can be studied under three major root causes of sociogenic, biogenic, and psychogenic. Also, the motives could be defined as intrinsic if the reason resides inside the criminal's psyche and extrinsic if it lies outside their psyche. Researchers have studied the behavior of the killers in detail to understand if the choices of the killer were made at random or were preplanned. Another factor that is studied in this regard is if the victim and the killer are strangers or related.

Copy Cat Approach

These studies have identified two major patterns used by the killers. There could be two possible reasons motivating a person with a sick mindset to kill as well as torture another human being.

One trend that is rather common among these individuals is that of the "Copy Cat." This is basically about their desire to be either feared or acknowledged. John Douglas described how this approach works in 1996. The serial killers, in their pursuit to be famous and feared, copy the actions of previous legendary serial killers.

The most popular example of this scenario is the BTK (Bind, Torture, Kill) strangler of Witchia, Kansas, whose role model for serial killings was Berkowitz. However, some people claim that the BTK incident had occurred before the time of Berkowitz but the similarities between the two indicate at least some level of connection.

Sexual Serial Killer

The other major type of serial killers is the sexual killer. These killers work in the most gruesome manner. A number of specialists including John Douglas have concluded after extensive research that the major trigger for a sexual serial killer is that of fantasy.

Studies suggest that in such cases, fantasy escalates to reality because of pornography. Other researchers emphasize that it is one of the most important factors if not the only one contributing to the increased instances of sexual killings. Pornography works as the fuel, building the inner desires of men that naturally exist inside them.

There are several statistics as well as real life cases indicating that the most dominant desire in men is that of sexual intercourse. Their psychology is naturally programmed in a manner that the act of penetration provides them satisfaction as they experience a sense of conquest and triumph.

However, unlike normal men, these serial killers do not get to learn about intimacy because of what they might have experienced in their pasts, especially during their childhood. As a result, their brain substitutesthe feeling of intimacy with that of control. Unfortunately, they fulfill their desire of obtaining control by inflicting physical harm to their victims. This translates as conquest in their sick minds, which somehow compensates for their inner desire of mating.

Many psychologists believe that the one thing that a serial killer pursues is control over others. This desire to conquer is rather strong in them because they do not have control over their own actions and its outcome. Consequently, in their quest to take control over others, they end up losing all control over themselves too.

Even though this sexual theme of serial killings is embraced by a huge number of researchers, Dr. Helen Morrison, who is a renowned psychotherapist disagrees with this theory altogether. She has interviewed several murderers and her final verdict is that the rate of sadomasochistic sex incidences is much higher than the cases of mass murders.

There are several theories regarding the motives of serial killers. Levin and Fox in 1985 discovered that the murderer's aim is to destroy the victim in order to experience triumph. Egger in 1985 believed that the motives of a serial killer are somewhat similar to that of rapists. In 1986, Leyton identified deprivation as the provocative trigger behind the frustration of a mass murderer. He had further stated that the mass murders are a semi-political protest by the killer that lands him a considerable profit in the form of fame, revenge, and sexual relief.

In the year 1972,Wilson had given an insight quite similar to that of Leyton's. He believed that when a person fails to find meaning beyond their daily routine, they are prone to become bitter, disgusted, and finally, violent. He said that when a society fails to provide an outlet for the passions of an idealist, they are bound to turn violent.

Norris described the serial killer syndrome behavior in 1988, in which he described 21 symptoms and patterns of aggression that provided a predisposition or a profile for a serial killer. Levin and Fox coined the famous terms "sociopath" and "psychopath" that are used a lot for describing serial killers in 1985. However, according to Dr. Helen Morrison, serial killer is a new personality type with different attributes than are witnessed in any other personality type.

Another of the most prominent theory that is discussed time and again in homicide literature is that of childhood trauma and inadequate socialization. These are indeed the leading cause of serial killings. Starr in 1972 had theorized that cruelty might play an important role in the creation of a serial killer. In the year 1975, Willie discovered that the most commonly occurring family background feature of the serial killers included violent punishment inflicted upon them in their childhood.

Lunde identified another more disturbing pattern in 1996, which comprised of either an unnatural or unusual relationship of the killer with their mothers. However, the most shocking discovery came in 1984, when Ressler found that several serial killers were fascinated by law enforcement.

Despite the extensive research that has been conducted in this field, there is still no definite answer to the question of what drives a serial killer's need to kill. There are a number of theories as we have explained in this chapter. A bad past, childhood issues, antisocial behavior, societal constraints, and a failure to fulfill sexual desires are among the most common reasons behind the development of a serial killer. However, at the end of the day, a serial murder is an independent act and individuals may have their own sets of reasons that motivate them to commit the acts of felony without feeling any remorse.

Chapter 4

Modus Operandi of Serial Killers— Methods and Patterns

We now have a detailed information about the driving forces of the serial murderers. This chapter will discuss in detail their methods and patterns of killing. The main aim of this study is to recognize the killing patterns, so that sufficient attempts could be made to stop them from happening.

Methods

Extensive studies have been conducted to study about the killing methods of the serial murderers. The former FRI agent Roy Hazelwood in this regard provided the most brilliant concept. He based his theory on the studies conducted by the famous FBI agents John Douglas and Robert Ressler. They had studied a total of 36 serial killers. He studied the cases in detail and developed a theory to classify serial murder crime scenes into an organized and disorganized dichotomy.

This theory uses the following factors to determine if the serial murder was an organized or disorganized crime:

- Was the victim was posed by the killer?
- Did the killer perform sexual acts on the victim either before or after death?
- Was the victim's body put through mutilation or cannibalism?

These factors are used to find out if the killer is an organized or a disorganized offender. This theory now makes the central part of the investigation of any serial murder.

Organized Offender

As per this famous dichotomy theory, if a particular homicide is an organized effort, little to no evidence will be found at the crime scene, as every move is preplanned and carefully premeditated. According to this classification theory, the organized serial killers could be psychopathic and antisocial but they are not insane. They are fully aware that they are committing a crime and yet they fail to show any remorse.

Organized serial killers are in most cases, attractive, employed, married or at last have a live-in partner, educated, possess above-average intelligence, orderly, cunning, skilled, and controlled. They are said to possess a certain level of charm and have the ability to talk their victims into their traps.

The case of an organized serial murder, you can expect at least three different crime scenes. There will be a first location, where the killer approached the victim. The nextone is the place where the victim was murdered, and finally a third location where they disposed of their body.

It is extremely difficult to catch the organized killers because they would always go to extreme lengths just for the sake of covering their tracks. Moreover, they are educated and intelligent people who are also well aware of the forensic procedure, which in turn means that they know and follow the investigation methods followed by the Police. Also, there is a high chance that they will be following the media and news reporting their crimes. In fact, they might correspond with the media as well.

Some of the most popular examples of organized killers include Joel Rifkin, Ted Bundy, and Dennis Rader.

Disorganized Offender

The disorganized serial murders are unplanned acts. Therefore, the criminals make the mistake of leaving behind evidences such as blood and fingerprint marks at the crime scene. Moreover, not much effort, is made to conceal or move the body of the victim. Such criminals are often young people who might be under the influence of drugs, alcohols, or are mentally ill. As opposed to the organized offenders, the disorganized killers are below average in terms of intelligence and possess deficient social skills or are deficient in communication.

A disorganized offender often comes from a dysfunctional or unstable family background. In some cases, such individuals have a history of being sexually or physically abused by their relatives. In some cases, these individuals are sexually uninformed, inhibited, or might have sexual aversions. A lot of them are compulsive masturbators. They are often socially isolated and are either confused or frightened when committing a murder. Some of them lack a means of reliable transportation as well and often kill their victims close to their own homes.

Their method of killing often includes "blitzing" of their victims, which corresponds to assaulting them suddenly with an overwhelming force. Such killers do not bother to remove the body of their victims from the location of murder. They simply make no attempt of hiding their victims. The classic example of a disorganized serial murderer is the famous Jack the Ripper.

Organized/Disorganized Murder

In some cases, the serial murder could be a mixture of organized and disorganized offence. This scenario usually happens when a number of people are involved in committing the murder. Since they have different personality types, it becomes difficult to classify the murder under a single category. In extremely rare cases, this could also happen when a lone serial killer undergoes a psychological transformation at different steps of his killing career.

Modus Operandi and Signature

The killing patterns of a serial killer are not only recognized by the organized/disorganized dichotomy. In addition to that, a serial killer might also leave traces of other behavioral patterns. The most popular behavioral patterns include MO (modus operandi) and signature. The modus operandi is a particular method used for killing a victim. On the other hand, a signature is the imprint or a personal mark left by the offender. While each crime has a modus operandi, signature may or may not be present.

The MO covers all the actions required to be performed by the criminal in order to complete the crime. For example, it covers points such as controlling the victim at the crime scene by tying them up. However, the MO, in most cases, is a practice that the criminal has learnt and is prone to changes as well, for example, with the experiences of the killer. A serial murderer like any other professional killer will modify and refine his methods. They could do it for various reasons, such as for adapting to new circumstances or for incorporating new information and skills. For example, instead of relying on the rope, a killer might learn that bringing handcuffs to the location of crime is a better and more time saving option. Attacking prostitutes with a knife on the streets at night was the popular MO of the most famous and the oldest serial killer, Jack the Ripper.

However, the signature is not a requirement of committing a serial murder. It only serves the psychological or emotional need of the criminal. The signature depicts the offender's psyche as such actions reflect their fantasy they might have for their prey. Such psychological fantasies develop over time and they heighten gradually. The most common and earliest manifestation of such psychological fantasies includes torturing the animals during their childhood. Dennis Rader, the infamous star behind the BTK (bind, torture, kill) case is the model example of this behavior.

What makes a signature unique is that if present, it is always the same. The reason behind this consistency is that it comes from deep within the offender's psyche. It has evolved a long time before they have committed their first murder. This signature act by the serial murders could be anything and often includes dismemberment or mutilation of the victim's body. For example, Jack the Ripper's signature included extensive mutilation and hacking of his prey's body. This characterized all the murders committed by him.

Staging or Posing

Several FBI profilers have witnessed scenarios where the crime scene has been deliberately altered. Mostly, the position of the victim's body is changed. Sometimes, these modifications are made for misleading the investigations and confusing the officials and investigators. If this is the case, such alterations come under the category of staging, and are considered as part of the criminal's MO.

In other cases, the alterations are made only for the purpose of serving the offender's fantasies. If this is the case, then such alterations are called posing. There are situations where the body of the victim is posed in a manner so as to send a message or a warning to the public and police. For example, Jack the Ripper's nude victims were the criminal's way of shocking the police and the onlookers in Victorian England.

While there are various examples of serial killings in the history, it has still been impossible to identify a particular pattern or method of killing. There are cases of serial killings where the psychology of the killers had a role to play, but serial murders without any signature moves have been witnessed as well. Therefore, it is rather hard to profile a serial killer with the information currently available.

Chapter 5

An Extensive look at the lives of Famous Serial Killers

Throughout the history, there have been various cases of serial killings. While some were extremely gruesome murders, others had psychological reasons behind them. Yet, there are a number of cases that might not have been reported at all or their culprits were never caught. In order to understand the psychology and circumstances of a serial killer, it is essential to study in detail as many cases as possible.

We have done extensive research to study the profiles of famous serial killers of the history. Here are the 5 killers and their disturbing acts discussed in detail:

1. Edmund Kemper

Edmund Kemper was responsible for killing six young women as well as some of his own family members. He was born on December 18, 1948. At the age of 15, he killed his grandparents just to know what it would feel to kill someone. When he was released from the prison for this offence, he began his career of picking up female hitchhikers and then releasing them afterwards. However, sometime later, he decided not to let them go and ended up murdering 6 women in the year 1970. The location for these murders was Santa Cruz, California. It was only in 1973 when he had murdered his own mother and her friend that he turned himself in.

Childhood Trauma

Edmund was born in Burbank, California, in the year 1948. He was the middle child of Clarnell and E.E. Kemper. In the year 1957, after the divorce of his parents, he moved to Montana with his two sisters and mother.

He had a disturbing childhood as he had to bear a difficult relationship with his mother, who was an alcoholic. She used to criticize him bitterly for his every move and he ended up blaming her for all of his problems. At the age of 10, she forced him to live in the basement. She wanted him to move away from his sisters so that he would not harm them in any way.

Edmund started showing signs of trouble early in life. He had dark fantasies, most of which circulated around him murdering his mother in the most brutal ways possible. He would cut off the heads of dolls that his sisters played with. Moreover, he would coerce girls into playing a twisted game with him that he would call "gas chamber." In this game, he asked the girls to blindfold him and make him sit in a chair. He would then pretend as if he was writhing in agony until he would pretend to 'die.'

The earliest stains of blood on his hand were that of his family cats. When he was 10 years old, he buried one of the cats alive while slaughtering the other one with a knife. He was sent to live with his father but then he ended up back with his mother anyway. Since she could not cope with him anymore, she decided to send him to live with his grandparents in North Fork, California.

Murdering his Grandparents

Kemper did not want to go and live at the farm of his grandparents but since he could not do anything about it, his rage kept on building. He had started searching and learning about firearms. His grandparents took his rifle away from him after he had shot various small animals and birds. Kemper had lava of anger boiling inside him, which turned on his grandparents. At the age of 15, he killed his grandmother after an argument, and then shot his grandfather. He hid the bodies after that.

What he had to say

After killing his paternal grandparents, he made a call to his mother. She told him to call the police and confess his crime to them. Later, Kemper told the police that he only shot his grandmother to find out what it felt like. His motive to kill his grandfather, according to him, was so that the man wouldn't have to find out about his wife.

The authorities handed him over to the California Youth Authority. After undergoing a number of tests, they found out that Kemper had an exceptionally high IQ. However, he was also diagnosed as suffering from paranoid schizophrenia. Finally, the authorities decided his destination to be Atascadero State Hospital that is a high security facility for convicts suffering from mental illnesses.

Kemper's Release

Kemper was 21 years old when he was released from the prison, in the year 1969. His prison doctor had clearly warned him against living with his mother due to her past behavior, since the psychological torture he had received from her could trigger his mental illness again. Yet, he went to live with her in Santa Cruz, California, where she had found a job at the University of California. She had recently ended her third marriage when he went to live with her. Kemper attended a community college for a while and did a number of jobs until he found employment, in 1971, with the Department of Transportation.

Kemper wanted to become a state trooper, but it was impossible because of his weight. He was 6 feet 9 inches tall and weighed around 300 pounds. It was because of his structure that he was given the nickname of "Big Ed". However, he would hang around with the police officers of Santa Cruz. One of them had given him handcuffs and a training school badge, while another had lent him his gun as well. Even his car looked like a police cruiser.

The year Kemper had started working with the highway department; a car hit him as he was on his motorcycle. When he filed a civil suit against the driver, he received a settlement of $15,000. As he was unable to work now, his mind started deviating towards other schemes. He started accumulating various weapons in his car that he had bought with the settlement money. He was planning to use them later for trapping women.

Edmund Kemper—the Co-ed Killer

At first, Kemper would only pick up these hitchhikers and then let them go. However, when two women, Mary Ann Pesce and Anita

Luchessa, accepted the lift he had offered them, they failed to make it to their destinations. Their families reported them to be missing but nothing was found until a female head was found in the woods, which was then identified as that of Pesce's. Kemper was not caught though. It was later found that he killed the women and brought the bodies to his home and had sexual intercourse with their corpses.

Kemper then killed Aiko Koo, Cindy Schall, Rosalind Thorpe, and Alice Liu. While he was out killing all these women, two other serial killers Herbert Mullins and John Linley Frazier were out killing people too. This won Santa Cruz the ignominious title of the "Murder capital of the world." As for Kemper, he was given the title of the "Co-ed Killer."

Murdering his Mother

In April of the year 1973, Kemper committed his final two murders. It was on a Good Friday that he had gone to his mother's house, where the two had a little fight. When she had gone to sleep, he attacked her by striking her in the head with a hammer, and then he slit her throat with a knife. He decapitated her as well as cut her, cut hands off, and removed her larynx and threw it in the garbage.

After disposing off her body, he called Sally Hallet, his mother's friend inviting her over to their house. He killed her as well and hid her body in the closet. He then fled from the area but upon reaching Pueblo, Colorado, he confessed his crimes to the Santa Cruz police.

The police did not believe that "Big Ed" was behind all the murders. He told them all about, the murders and found that all the evidence matched his stories.

Trial

In October of 1973, Kemper was charged with and tried for eight first-degree murders. In early

November, he was found guilty of every charge. When the judge asked him how he should be punished, Kemper said that, they should torture him to death. The judiciary, however, proved to be less cruel than he wished them to be and they decided on eight concurrent life sentences, which he served at the California Medical Facility in Vacaville.

2. Jack Unterweger

Jack Unterweger, an Austrian serial murderer, killed a number of women. He was born on August 16, 1950, in Austria, and died in 1994 when he committed suicide.

Early Life

Unterweger was born in Styria, Austria. As a child, his prostitute mother abandoned him. He was forced to live with his alcoholic grandfather. His criminal career started when he was in his teens. He was arrested for assaulting an 18-year-old prostitute at the age of 16.

Writer and a Killer

Unterweger was convicted for murdering Margaret Schaefer in 1976. He was sentenced to a life imprisonment. It was in the prison that he learned to read and write. The activity instilled in him a love for literature, and his flair for writing impressed a number of people both inside and outside the jail.

He wrote an autobiography, *Fegefeuer oder die Reise ins Zuchthaus* (*Purgatory or the Trip to Jail - Report of a Guilty Man*) in 1984 that turned out to be a best-seller. His literary convictions and behavior convinced the state that he had repented and was a reformed man and he was released, in 1990, on parole.

After his release from the prison, he received the status of a literary celebrity and appeared on talk shows as well. His best-seller was turned

into a movie and he went on to become a
journalist.

Murders and Suicide

While he had been putting on an impressive
show for the world, people were still suspicious
of his transformation. As a number of
prostitutes were found dead with an MO similar
to that of the Schaefer murder, the police
decided to put him on surveillance. They did
impressive detective work for several months,
and soon they had evidence sufficient enough
to arrest him.

He was detained in the year 1992 and he
continued to proclaim his innocence giving
interviews to the media. He called upon his
literary colleagues for help and some even
came forward too. However, his charming
personality and carefully-crafted pleas of
innocence were of no use, since the evidence
against him was sufficient and he was found

guilty of committing 9 murders. He was
sentenced to a lifetime of imprisonment in the
year 1994, but he committed suicide by hanging
himself using a string from his prison garment.

3. Gary Ridgway

Gary Ridgway was an American serial killer. He
had been found guilty of killing 49 people.
However, he confessed of killing double that
amount, possibly around 90. However, the
other murders were not proved. He was termed
the most prolific American murderer in history
because of the number of murders he had
committed.

Early Life

Ridgway was born on February 18, 1949, in
Utah. He was the middle child of Mary and
Thomas Ridgway and had two brothers. He had
a troubled life at home, as his mother was
described as somewhat domineering. His
parents argued quite a lot, which probably had

a negative effect on his psyche. Ridgway had an I.Q of 82. He committed his first felony at the age of 16, stabbing a boy of 6 years old. He had directed the boy to the woods and stabbed him into his liver. The boy had survived the attack though.

The Green River Killer

Gary Leon Ridgway was given the title of "Green River Killer." For over 20 years, he had haunted the Pacific Northwest. His major targets were helpless female runways from around the Seattle area, as well as sex workers.

His MO included strangling them by hand. He would then bury their bodies somewhere along the Green River or around the forest. In most cases, he returned to the victim's body to have sexual intercourse with it. He kept on operating until 2001, when DNA profiling revealed his connection to these eccentric murders. He was charged for murdering 49 women, but he confessed to have killed around 90. He was sentenced to a lifetime imprisonment in the federal prison of Colorado.

4. John Bodkin Adams

Dr. John Bodkin Adams is famous for his involvement in the extremely suspicious deaths of 163 people all of whom turned out to be his former patients. Adams belonged to Randallstown in Ireland. He was born on January 21, 1899. He was not a very successful doctor but his elderly patients continually placed his name in their wills. He was also infamous for using medications that were extremely dangerous, and were not to be used until necessary. This practice along with the death of 163 of his former patients raised the suspicions of the police. However, he was not found guilty of the charges at the trial.

The Crimes of Dr. Adams

Dr. Adams' case remains one of the most controversial ones among all the serial killings documented because of the fact that he was never found guilty at the trial. The mystery still shrouds the case even after his death. While some people think that his practices had inspired the infamous medical mass murderer, Harold Shipman, the others are of the opinion that he was simply carrying out mercy killings, as at that time the only way to alleviate terminal suffering was with painkillers.

Despite not being an exceptionally recognized practitioner, the doctor was preferred by many elderly patients because of his considerate and compassionate behavior towards them. The investigators, however, were more concerned about his modus operandi as he used dangerous drugs and took a pathological interest in the wills of his patients.

His victims included Edith Alice Morrell who suffered from a stroke and was partially paralyzed. Dr. Adams gave her a mixture of heroine and morphine to ease her pain. She added clauses to her will where he was to receive money after her death. However, she added another clause three months before her death, according to which, he was not to receive anything. However, he was given cutlery, some money, and a Rolls Royce. He maintained that she had died of natural causes.

His other famous victim was Gertrude Hullett. The story goes that she lost consciousness in his presence and he called for an autopsy even though she was still alive. This showed his incompetence as a doctor and it was the local pathologist Francis Camps who realized that the poor woman was still alive. However, she died later and Adams recorded brain hemorrhage to be the cause of her death. However, an official investigation revealed that she had committed suicide. Mysteriously enough, she left a number of valuable items in her will for the doctor, which included a Rolls Royce as well.

Trial and Investigation

After the death of Mrs. Hullet, the word on the street was that this Doctor was an angel of death. The gossip was strong enough to stir the suspicions of local police as well as the media, and they confronted Dr. Adams after an extensive investigation of several months, in the year 1956.

In his defense, Adams said that relieving a patient from their pain is not a crime. However, all his deceased patients continuously left him valuable items and money in their wills, which made it impossible for the police to believe his stories.

In March 1957, his trial took place. His defense made the point that the only evidence against him was the nurses who were appointed by him for tending Mrs. Morrell. Most of these nurses claimed that the doctor gave her dangerously high dosage of potentially risky medications. However, as it so happened, they had the record of the dosages in journals. When these were examined, they turned out to be in the normal ranges for a terminally ill patient. Apparently, the nurses were influenced by the local gossip when they had given their verbal evidence against the doctor. Moreover, only one of the two medical experts on the jury called it a murder. The defense then provided evidence that he was not a reliable witness either.

The defense lawyer of Dr. Adams made sure that he was not forced to appear in the witness box and that none of the evidence from the Hullett's case was used, especially the testimony of the nurse who had tended her. This particular nurse had been reported to tell the doctor, "You do realize doctor, that you have killed her?"

It took the jury only 45 minutes to find the doctor not guilty of the murder. The trial ended on April 15, 1957 and by the year 1961, he was allowed to continue his practice as a general practitioner as well. However, the police and the public continued to condemn him for the murders until the day of his death on July 4, 1983. His fortune at the time of his death was worth 402,970 pounds, as he continued to receive legacies from his patients until his death.

5. Myra Hindley

Myra Hindley was a serial killer whose victims were small children. She committed these crimes in partnership with her boyfriend, Ian Brady. She was an English murderess and, along with her boyfriend, she would rape her victims before killing them. Her 17 years old brother reported off her in law. She had pleaded not guilty to all the murders she was charged for, but they found her guilty of committing at least three of those murders. She was sentenced to life imprisonment and she died in the jail, in the year 2002.

Early Life

Hindley was born on July 23, 1942 in Manchester, England. She lived with her grandmother. At the age of 15, she decided to leave school after the death of a close friend. Then, she converted to Roman Catholicism. It was in the year 1961 that she met Ian Brady, her future boyfriend. He was a stock clerk who was released from the prison recently. Soon, she found herself falling in love with him to the point that he controlled her every movement.

Murders

Brady, in his quest to test the level of her allegiance, planned rapes and murders of children. It was in the month of July in 1963 that they committed their first felony. Their victim was Pauline Reade. Only four months after that, they claimed their next victim who was a 12 year old boy named John Kilbride. Then came the murder of Keith Bennett in June of 1964. Finally, their fourth reported victim was Lesley Ann Downey, a 10-year-old girl who was kidnapped from the local fairground.

Tip off

In October of the year 1965, David Smith— Hindley's brother-in-law, alerted the police about the duo's crimes. He had witnessed the murder of Edward Evans, whom Brady had killed with an axe. He told the police that Brady had mentioned that he had buried more bodies on the Saddleworth Moor.

Trial

Brady and Hindley were tried on April 27, 1966. Both of them pleaded not guilty and refused to accept the charges of any of the murders committed by them. However, Hindley was found guilty of murdering Evans and Downey, while Brady was found guilty of murdering Kilbride, Downey, and Evans. Both of them were sentenced to life imprisonment.

We have discussed only 5 murderers in the history of the serial killings. However, the examples are numerous and most of them are extremely gruesome with most of the killers following a hair-raising modus operandi. In these cases, you could see that most of the killers had faced some kind of trauma in their childhood. This theme is consistent with several of the other serial killers as well. Another trend that is common among serial killers is their obsession with sex. As was the case with Unterweger, some of them harbor a deep hatred against prostitutes, a theme followed by the first officially reported killer, Jack the Ripper. However, some psychologists would argue that it was more because of his mother being a prostitute that he chose them to be the targets for his crime. Seldom is the motive behind the serial killings to gain some kind of benefit, as was the case with Dr. Adams. Another common theme is that of suicide. Since many of these murderers are aware of what they are doing, they often end up either committing suicide or confessing to their crimes. Yet, there are a large number of killers who feel no remorse and are convinced of their own innocence. In the next chapter, we will further discuss the psychology and environment of these killers. Many of the female serial killers worked in healthcare fields with nursing being the most common one. Kristen Gilbert, also known by the title Angle of Death, committed three first degree murders. Her modus operandi included injecting the victims with epinephrine. She was a nurse by occupation and her victims were her patients. Jane Toppan was another female serial killer who was a nurse and practiced the art of killing her responsible for their behaviors

Historical Fact

The first record of a group of serial killers goes back to the Roman Empire. According to reports, it was a group of matrons who had poisoned their prey by means of a deadly ring.

Chapter 6

Sociopath vs. Psychopath

When it comes to serial killers, most people assume that something is wrong with their minds. Thus, the most commonly researched field concerning them is their criminal minds. Therefore, they are usually characterized as psychopaths. However, there is a fine line between two important terms, psychopath, and sociopath that are often used interchangeably in literature. If we are to understand the criminal mind to even the smallest extent, we must learn to differentiate between these two terms.

No doubt there are certain characteristics that the two phenomenon share. These include the following:

- A general disregard for social norms and laws

- Aloof to other people's rights on them
- No guilt or remorse for what they do
- Violent behavior

However, the two kinds of personalities show a number of dissimilarities as well. We will discuss what makes a psychopath different from a sociopath in the following paragraphs:

Following the extensive research on the topic, the sociopaths were found to be extremely nervous people who are easy to agitate. They are emotionally unstable and are prone to outbursts, such as fits of rage. According to some studies, sociopaths have underprivileged backgrounds and are often less educated. They might fail to adhere to a job for long and face problems in staying at one place for long. While they find it hard to form attachments with other people, it is not entirely impossible for them. They could, however, form attachments to a particular person or even a group of people, but they usually do not have any regard of the society in general. They have an extremely disturbed life pattern, which also reflects in their actions. The crimes committed by them, including the murder, are bound to belong to the disorganized category. It will be an act of spontaneity and is never going to be a planned action.

A serial murderer, according to the classic definition of Levin and Fox, is after that feeling of superiority that taking the life of another individual is bound to bring to them. This is because of their extreme need to control and seek power that often leads them to such behaviors. This kind of behavior also gives them a sense of social glorification.

However, psychopaths have a few habits that belong to the opposite end of the spectrum than that of a sociopath's. While they are not easily unnerved and some psychopaths exhibit extremely charming personality traits, they fail to form emotional attachments with people in their surroundings. Moreover, they could never show even a trace of empathy to their victims or to people in general.

Psychopaths have an extremely manipulative demeanor and they know exactly how to gain other people's trust. Despite the fact that they are unable to harbor genuine feelings for their fellow humans, they are smart enough to know how to mimic other people's emotions. Therefore, an unsuspecting individual wouldn't be able to tell the difference between a psychopath and a normal individual. Also, unlike sociopaths, these individuals are educated people with steady jobs. In rare cases, they are so good at what they do that they could mimic their way to long-term relationships and have families as well. They are extremely smart people and never let a shroud of doubt enter in the minds of their near and dear ones regarding their diseased minds.

When it comes to deciding what category a serial killer belongs to, the line between a sociopath and a psychopath becomes hazy. Some of the researchers studying this field believe that a serial killer is neither a sociopath nor a psychopath, but has characteristics of their own that might belong to either category. However, there are others who believe that serial killers have a greater tendency towards being a sociopath.

Therefore, considerable research has been conducted to study the sociological factors affecting a serial killer. These factors include those related to societal norms and culture. Leyton discovered the classic theory that came out from this extensive research in 1986. According to him, indulging in a series of murders gives the killer a sense of triumph. It gives them satisfaction as they feel they are being a part of a conservative and sociopolitical protest to gain a sense of revenge identity, fame, and in some cases sexual relief.

On the same note, Sear discovered that societal norms play a crucial role in the creation of a serial killer. According to this theory, one of the main reasons why people become serial killers is because society has assigned specific roles to men and women where men are supposed to be powerful, strong, and unemotional and women must be submissive and weak. As the statistics show, the majority of the serial killers are male and only a negligible number of female serial killers are witnessed. These males think that by killing, they are showing their strength, which is the role that society gave them to begin with. While Sear's theory is ideal for proving a few cases, it does not hold true in several other scenarios. This is why other researchers have come up with their own theories.

The other famous theory related to serial killers is that of Mitchell's. He based his theory on societal norms and ideas put forward by Hirschi in his work in the year 1969. In his work, he had explored the fundamental relationships between man and his society. According to his work, in addition to the societal roles expected of a particular gender, there are other bonds that an individual has with their society based on their commitment and attachments.

Attachment between two individuals means that they are sensitive to each other's perception about themselves. However, in case of commitment, there is a social reward that is connected to their conforming to the laws and norms of the society.

A normal individual has both a number of attachments as well as commitments to their society. However, a serial killer often fails to form or receive any form of attachment or commitment. Such people often live with a perpetual sense of isolation from their society, which is the main factor responsible for creating anomalies in their behaviors.

Sears provided another theory that is generally accepted and is still prevalent among researchers. He was of the opinion that media has an extremely important role to play in the development of a serial killer. He thought that pornography is a major driving force in the creation of these brutes--especially the sexual fanatic types of killers. In addition to pornography, the extreme aggression and violence shown on the media are also leading factors behind creating such monsters in the society. In fact, researchers have found out that there is a strong correlation between the numbers of violent incidents in the society and media. Since human beings are inherently programmed to mimic their surroundings, it is in their genes to look for a role model. The media with its violent heroes provides those role models readymade to be mimicked and followed.

The most popular examples of this scenario include movies such as Henry: The Portrait of a Serial Killer" and the Silence of the Lambs" While these are extremely entertaining and have a huge fan following, there is no point in arguing that these could be educational for someone who has tendencies of becoming a serial killer.

Differential Association

Mitchell further supported Sear's theory about media and pornography being responsible for the creation of serial killers in a concept that he called as "differential association." This is a different version of Sear's theory as it states that people learn criminal behavior by forming primary group relationships as opposed to learning it from secondary sources. The same idea was accepted and propagated by Sutherland in 1937 as well. According to this theory, most serial killers learn about advanced murder techniques from other inmates in prison as they are imprisoned for other crimes before attempting their first murder. This pattern is confirmed by studying a number of real life cases as well for many serial killers that have a history of being jailed for minor crimes or for attempting murder while being a juvenile.

Pornography acts in a similar manner too. It fuels the imagination of over sexualized people. As most of these serial killers have trouble forming interpersonal relationships, they harbor an insatiable appetite for sexual activities for which they turn to pornography instead. Researchers are of the opinion that since most of the pornographic material portrays women and children in submissive roles, these serial killers get ideas for their techniques to inflict torture in similar ways.

Mitchell did a lot of research concerning the sociological aspects responsible for creating serial killers. He specifically researched those areas of culture and societal norms that are bound to create such monsters and has developed two major theories to study its correlation with the serial murders. We have discussed both the theories in detail below.

Functionalist/Structural Approach

Mitchell has modeled this theory after Durkheim's work, which is about crime, deviance, and the breakdown in the social consensus of societal values and goals. He further argued that our society is drifting away from a common societal objective. According to him, serial killers are unable to keep up with the changes occurring in the society and, as they feel helpless with nothing under their control, they choose violence as their only outlet.

Social Ends and Means

This second theory of Mitchell's is somewhat similar to the first one except it deals with social ends and means. He debates that in a society while some people may have higher aspirations and goals, others might not be as ambitious. However, the current structure of the culture is such that it promotes only success and achievement. As these virtues are celebrated above all else, there are other people who fail to be successful or even pursue success as the final end, which ultimately puts a strain on them. As a result of this continuous pressure, such individuals might turn to illegal and brutal means to achieve success. They find a sense of enlightenment by performing acts that are vile and dishonest. For a serial killer, the means to achieve a sense of triumph is via violence and killing.

Family Issues

Apart from the role played by the media and the changing structure of the society, a major factor that is responsible for making huge sociological and psychological changes for an individual that might turn them into a serial killer is family issues. Having serious unresolved family issues can create gaps in an individual's personality that are impossible to fill. Moreover, people who have witnessed continuous episodes of violence in their childhood are more likely to turn to violence in time of desperation than someone who has never been through such a struggle. Brutality and sadism are said to have deep influence on serial murderers. Various authors have found out a significant correlation between aggression and serial killings.

Starr in 1972 discovered that human cruelty could be the reason behind the development of serial killers. In 1975, Willie revealed that the most recurring family background feature among serial killers was violent punishments in their childhood. Holmes and DeBurger in 1988 then explored the two of the most common socio-cultural sources that play an important role in influencing the behavior of these serial killers. These factors include persistence of violence in the society as well as the effects of violence in a family setting as experienced during the early years of childhood. They consider both of these factors to have a major contribution in the creation of such monsters in the society.

Next came the findings of Scott that show even that if childhood abuse does not create a direct link to the occurrence of a crime in future, it still forms an undeniable factor that was shared by an enormous number of serial killers. Moreover, the most commonly blamed culprit for childhood abuse scenario has been the mother. However, in 2000, Scott reported that, in a lot of cases, it is the sadistic and disciplinarian fathers popping in the serial murderers family tree that are responsible for the creation of such monsters in the society.

Home Environment

There are several correlations found between the home environment and the development of a serial killer. In a study conducted in the year 1985, the Federal Bureau of Investigations found out that a majority of the serial killers had experienced uncaring, unhealthy, and abusive home environments.

This theme was also validated by the studies conducted by Sears. He found that there was a prevailing absence of a nurturing and loving relationship between these serial killers and their parents during their childhood. Further studies have concluded that people who had experienced abuse as children are more likely to exhibit violent behavior.

Sears, however, had provided the world with a more comprehensive angle on the topic. According to his theory, the absence of a nurturing behavior increases an individual's chances of becoming a sociopath. It paves way for insecurities and such individuals often show behaviors that are a product of low self-esteem. They do not know how to interact with people around them and, therefore, they fail to form attachments or have long-term relations. This makes them frustrated and they feel helpless. Not being able to fulfill what they think they are supposed to do, they turn to other ways to fulfill their desires. This results in their violent behavior at times.

There are several theories about what goes inside the minds of these criminals, but there is no way to determine the pattern for every serial killer out there. While many share some characteristics, there are others who act in a completely different manner. This difference occurs because serial killing, in most of the cases, is an individual act and thus it is highly difficult to predict the behavior as they are bound to have different backgrounds, reasons, and methods of killings. However, we have tried to study the pattern that has been found to be the most popular among the killers.

As far as the personality type of a serial killer is concerned, there is no way to give a definite answer in this regard. There are a lot of serial murderers in the past that have been identified as sociopaths by the researchers. In fact, there are not many serial killers who can be classified as psychopaths and the idea has been more prevalent because of the media rather than research based on facts and figures. However, there are cases where the individuals are neither sociopaths nor psychopaths but a mixture of the two. This is why a number of researchers have concluded that serial killers might have a personality type of their own which is distinct from other types of personalities.

Every individual showing the signs of being a sociopath might end up becoming a serial killer. Instead of targeting anyone who might have a slightly different personality, efforts should be made to improve the structure of the society and preach about the importance of developing tolerance in the society towards what slightly deviates from the societal norms. Meanwhile, people who show tendencies towards violence and have aggressive behavior should be helped and if their behaviors are a result of any kind f psychosis, they must be treated accordingly.

Chapter 7

Identifying a Serial Killer

Identifying a serial killer, especially before they start committing murders, is a rather difficult task that requires a lot of researching and practice. You need to understand the psychology of people before even suspecting an individual of having such tendencies. In the previous section, we have explored the psychology of serial killers. In this section, we will further delve into the backgrounds of famous serial killers in order to identify their characteristic behaviors. This can be of significance when identifying a potential serial killer.

There are several cases when people, upon finding that a certain person has committed murders and is identified as a serial killer, are extremely surprised. They find it hard to believe that a perfectly normal person who they think they knew very well could even be capable of committing such gruesome acts. This is because most of the serial killers learn to act normal when they are in company. In fact, some of them hide behind a façade of charming personalities and nice manners.

Predicting the Killers

While there is no certain way to indicate that a particular person is or will become a serial killer, there are still some signs that can help us find people who have the highest potential to commit such crimes. Some of these signs do not include violence, but there is a strong correlation between the two.

Antisocial Behavior

One of the most common characteristics shared by various serial killers is antisocial behavior. Antisocial personality disorder is identified as a mental disorder and people suffering from this condition are likely to show no guilt for their actions, fail to conform to societal standards, are compulsive liars, show irresponsibility, and in some cases, they even resort to aggression. However, not every antisocial person grows to become a serial killer. The presence of a few other signs is crucial if a person is to be suspected or investigated without any evidence.

Example of Antisocial Behavior

John Wayne Gacy was a serial killer who became famous for murdering and raping 33men and teenage boys. However, he had no remorse for committing these crimes. He went on to call his victims "worthless little queers and punks."

Voyeurism

Voyeurism is among the other eccentric behaviors identified by criminologists as the driving force behind the serial killings. This not only appeals to the diseased minds of these individuals as an act to derive sexual pleasure from, but also acts as a means to have full control over other people's lives. As they violate the privacy of another person they tend to enjoy a sense of control over their victims.

According to studies, a great number of serial killings started off as petty sexual crimes. The killer's addiction with such behavior advances to the stage of assault and murder after a while as they attempt to satiate their passions. Stalking their prey gives them an advantage as they learn their behaviors and routines in private settings. This makes such killings a success. However, it is not difficult to sense if a particular individual is keeping a tab on you. All you need to do is pay a little more attention to your surroundings. This especially stands true for women, as they are the most common victims for the voyeurism related murders.

Example of Voyeurism

Danny Rolling is a classic example of this type of behavior. He was caught several times spying on cheerleaders when they were bathing or dressing at the campus. His peers knew perfectly well that he was a peeping Tom and acted as witnesses later when their friend killed eight of the local students. All of the killings were sexually motivated.

Neglect and Childhood Abuse

If there is any one behavior that is shared most commonly by a staggering number of serial killers, it is a traumatic childhood. For some, it was riddled with verbal abuse, while others were the victims of physical as well as sexual abuse. According to a study conducted by the FBI, a somewhat similar pattern of harsh childhood full of neglect was common among the dozens of serial killers interviewed by them.

Being neglected by the closest people during one's childhood is bound to have severe repercussions in the personalities of such individuals. This matters because there are several stages of development during the childhood that play a crucial role in learning about empathy, love, and how to interact with other people. For some individuals, it becomes nearly impossible to learn these traits later in life if they are not imprinted on their minds during their childhoods.

Example of Childhood abuse

Aileen Wurnos was a prostitute who killed6 of her clients. She was abandoned by her mother right before her 4th birthday. She was left to live with and be raised by her maternal grandparents. However, this living arrangement turned into a life full of horrors and abuse for her. Aileen's grandfather was a monster who not only sexually abused her, but also left her to be raped by his friends.

These attacks left her pregnant when she was only 14 years old. She gave birth to the baby at a facility for unwed mothers, where she was forced to give her child away. When she turned 15, her grandmother died and her grandfather threw her out. She turned to prostitution for her survival.

Poor Performance at work and academics

Most of the serial killers have a high IQ and are generally above average when it comes to intelligence. These people handle the complicated logistics of murdering a lot of people and then get away with it too. Even if they are caught ultimately, it is in most cases because of their need for killing again and again. There are others who just surrender for the sake of recognition and fame. This proves that serial killers are not dumb.

If they are intelligent individuals, how come most of them are unable to show progress in their careers? In fact, a lot of them remain unemployed for several months at a stretch. The reason behind their failure to have successful careers is their incapacity to mix together with others and their inability to respect the social norms and rules. Therefore, another major sign that an individual might have tendencies of becoming a serial killer is their consistently poor academic record or work progress despite being intelligent.

Example

There is no way to avoid the name of famous serial killer Ted Bundy when it comes to the topic of serial murders. He murdered at least 30 people and was reported to have an IQ of136. However, this was not enough to allow him a distinguished academic record. In fact, he dropped out of two universities before he finally settled for a string of menial jobs that were often low paying. It did not bother him either since his life's purpose was to kidnap and kill women.

Obsession and Fantasizing

This may not be the most common occurrence among the serial killers, but there are still a number of cases where these individuals, remain haunted by their twisted and violent sexual desires that are unlikely to ever develop into an obsession for depraved fantasies. These sick fantasies of theirs are often accompanied by masturbation. This happens particularly because these killers are unable to form similar relationships with actual people.

Example

Andrei Chikatilo, also recognized as 'Rostov Ripper', was a sexual serial killer. He was reported to have masturbated so violently and frequently that his penis was severely scarred.

Head Injuries

When anybody fails to slightly conform to the societal standards, people often say joking that he must have been dropped on his head as a child. However, head injuries are not a laughing matter at all. The chances of developing a violent behavior with increased aggression are higher if the pre-frontal cortex is damaged. This part of the brain is responsible for planning and making judgments. Therefore, an injury to this part plays a crucial role in messing with the judgments of an individual.

Example

The notorious killer, Richard Ramirez, who was also famous as the Night Stalker, had sustained two serious head injuries during his childhood. At the age of two, a dresser had fallen on his head resulting in injuries that required 30 stitches. When Ramirez turned five years old, a swing at the local park knocked him unconscious. Criminologists believe that these injuries might have damaged his frontal lobe.

Bedwetting

Bedwetting is a common problem among kids. However, it usually persists until the age of 5. If the children persistently wet their beds even after entering their teenage years then it is definitely an alarming matter that needs consideration. Such a situation in fact indicates the presence of medical conditions, such as psychological unrest, trauma, and neuroses. In fact, these are the symptoms of a diseased mind and such conditions are common among the criminals such as swindlers, murderers, and especially serial killers.

Example

The blood-chilling example of a classic bedwetting serial killer is the famous Alton Coleman. Reportedly, he was a consistent bed wetter to the point that his peers had named him "pissy." He went on to kill seven people before the authorities caught him.

Arson

If you are looking for signs to identify a serial killer, a deep interest in setting fires is a dead giveaway. While the argument remains that many people, especially youngsters, enjoy the site of flames as they mirror their inner passion, the fact remains that an unusual interest in arson should raise a considerable level of suspicion for sure. A psychopath with a serious tendency to kill is a potential arsonist. They enjoy the activity to such an extent that they would not mind setting everything they see on fire. Pyromania is usually common among potential serial murderers. It only makes sense to a twisted mind to love the uncontrollable acts of destruction and find them fascinating.

Example

Ottis Toole, the murderer of at least 6 people, was an arsonist before he became a murderer. He loved to set things on fire as its destructive power sexually aroused him.

Torturing Animals

Killing animals for no reason is another type of behavior that can be related to serial killing. Such behavior includes the torturing, provoking, or even killing of dogs, cats, and other animals. Another characteristic behavior of potential serial murderers or psychopaths in general is their failure to feel any guilt or remorse even after witnessing the results of their actions.

Basically, serial killers seek control over others, and when they are still young, the only kind of creature they can completely dominate include small animals. Such behavior indicates they are at a risk of becoming serial killers on reaching adulthood.

Example

There are number of examples of people who used to kill and torture small animals during their adolescent years and grew up to become dangerous serial killers. However, Jeffrey Dahmer is an unusually infamous case. He had impaled the head of a dog on a stick and left it in full view for people to see the grotesque scene.

These are some of the classic behaviors that are often shown by serial killers before they finally turn to the gruesome career of preying on living souls. While it is important to know that not all the people who indulge in these or similar acts will later become serial killers, these are some general indicators of a potentially sick mind. Therefore, if people portray acts of similar nature accompanied with a cold, remorseless behavior, they should be put under surveillance. I do not, in any circumstances, promote the usage of violence to control the situation as violence only begets violence. However, if such anomalous behavior is detected, such people should be immediately given attention in order to make up for what they lack in their personalities.

By paying sufficient attention to our surroundings, we can save not only the victims, but several people could be prevented from becoming monstrous criminals. Considering the importance of this subject, the next chapter is also dedicated to studying the anomalous behavior of such criminals, but from a different angle.

Chapter 8

Anomalous Behavior

In the previous chapter, we discussed the earliest signs of budding serial killers. However, in this section we will be throwing some light on the traits that are surely present in adult serial killers. Criminologists have studied these individuals in details to identify the traits that are characteristically shown by these criminals.

The Five Major Signs shown by a Serial Killer

When it comes to spotting a serial murderer, the criminologists have identified the following five major traits that a number of most notorious criminals and serial killers have in common:

- Manipulative Individuals
- Charming personalities
- Power hungry

- Egotistical
- Appear to be an average Joe

Making use of the most advanced technology, criminologists and psychologists have identified and defined the circumstances that make someone stoop to the level of committing cold murders--not once, but over and over again.

Dr. Elizabeth Yardley, who is a famous name in the world of psychology and criminology and is the Director of the Center for Applied Criminology at Birmingham City University, has highlighted five of the key characteristics of a serial killer that we have mentioned above. Let us delve deeper in these traits so as to identify a serial killer more easily and more definitely.

1. Sign no. 1—A Power Junkie

According to experts, "most of the serial killers have a strong hunger for power, even when they are caught and know very well that the game is up for them." However, this desire to have a control over the situation often turns out to be their undoing. Their intent to have immense control over the people and situation makes them hold back important bits of crucial information. In their bid to have power and control over the situation, they end up drawing too much attention to themselves. In their attempts to keep their warped sense of authority, they fail to realize that they have lost the game.

A classic example of this kind of behavior is Ian Brady. He and his accomplice, Myra Hindley, who are famous as the Moors murderers were convicted for murdering five children. These murders took place between the years 1963 and 1965. He was adamant to not disclose the location of one of their victims, Keith Bennett's body. The modern psychologists are of the belief that he had done so only to assert control and power.

2. Sign no. 2 — A Dangerous Manipulator

The experts on criminology and serial killers believe that one trait that is shared among various serial killers is their capacity to hide their sinister personality behind showing traits such as a need to please and apparent vulnerability.

In fact, many of the world's most famous and ingenious serial killers were frighteningly adept at manipulating the people around them. They somehow knew which buttons to press with which individual that will portray them in just the right light. These individuals are also capable of manipulating situations in such a way that their actions could be blamed on the society. Moreover, some of them are intelligent and cunning to the point of using the modern medical psychological research for explaining and even justifying their actions.

A horrific example of this behavior is Doctor Harold Shipman. He would use his position as a medical practitioner to manipulate the patients into opting of fatal treatments--all such grotesque actions while maintaining the stature of a caring member of the society.

3. Sign no. 3 — an Egotistical Bragger

As per detailed studies carried out by many psychologists, many serial killers are after attentions and fame. This theme is present in a number of cases of serial murders. Many studies have confirmed that the brain of this type of person is wired in a way that they cannot help but brag about the mayhem they have caused. They brag about their crimes to anybody who is interested, or is forced to listen. These include their victims, accomplices, and law enforcement personnel. Some had even been reported to brag of their 'achievements' to themselves.

An example of this situation is the duo Brady and Hindley who would revisit Saddle worth Moor—the burial sites of their victims in order to collect ghoulish shots of the desolate area just to keep the memories of their horrendous crimes.

However, their behavior end up giving them away and the police finally found the bodies of their three victims on the Moor. Similarly, Trevor Hardy, who was a convicted British serial murderer, was caught only because he had bragged about one of his victims to his younger brother. He was widely known as Beast of Manchester and used to murder teenage girls.

4. Sign no. 4 — A Superficial Charmer

Another characteristic that is often depicted by potential serial killers is their superficial charm. They have a tendency to identify other people's emotions and quickly grasp their weaknesses and vulnerabilities. They use their findings later into coaxing these people into doing what they normally would not have done.

Research has confirmed what Dr. Yardley believes to be true as well, that serial killers with these traits get their victims on side and bring them under their control utilizing a mixture of common sense and compliments.

The classic example of this type of personality is the famous serial killer, Ted Bundy. He was executed in the year 1989 when he confessed to murdering 30 people in 7 different states between the years 1974 and 1978. However, popular belief is that he had actually killed a lot more people than that. His modus operandi included winning the trust of women before kidnapping, raping, and killing them. He did that by either faking disability with fake casts and slings or by pretending to be a person of authority such as a police officer. He was described as a handsome man with a charismatic and charming personality.

5.   Sign no. 5 — an Average Joe

At first glance, many of the serial killers seem to be nothing more than an average Joe. In fact, some of them appear to be a pillar of the community. This is the scariest trait of any serial killer because it makes it impossible to identify them.

This is nothing more than their method of gaining trust so they would abuse it later in the most appalling way possible. This tactic has been more successful than acquiring false manners and charms and a number of deviant activities have been committed behind closed doors thanks to their ability to gain people's trust quickly.

Here is an example of this kind of behavior. Inhabitants of a residential street of Gloucester in the UK, the duo—Fred and Rose--acted as if they were like any other normal family. However, between the years 1967 and 1987, the pair went to torture and rape girls and young women. They killed around 12 where many of their victims were family members. They buried the bodies in their garden.

Another example of a similar scenario is John Wayne Gacy, an American serial murderer, who was nicknamed as "Killer Clown." He was a politically active citizen from Chicago suburb. He worked hard for the betterment of his local community and performed as 'Pogo the clown" at events and parties. Unfortunately, this rosy side was only one of the many facets of his twisted personality. In his private hours, he raped and then murdered young boys and buried their bodies in the grounds of his house.

These are the 5 major personality types that are often attributed to serial killers. However, the anomalous behavior characteristics of such killers could be a result of various social and psychological factors as we have already discussed in the previous sections. Various studies have shown that people who come from unstable and broken families most commonly show anomalous behavior showing an unusual interest in acts such as sadomasochism and voyeurism from an early age.

The negative behavior is so ingrained in the nature of these people that they actually stand by their actions and justify them to anyone who would care to listen. Charles Manson, who is famous for taking the lives of 7 people in only two nights in the year 1969, reportedly made an alarming statement. He said that if given the chance, he would "like to encourage violence among children at school". Many believe that his mindset was a product of facing neglect and abuse when he was a child.

It is, however, important to note that childhood abuse and unstable families are not always the reasons behind the creation of these monsters. For example big names among the serial killers such as Jeff Dahmer— a Milwaukee Cannibal, Dennis Rader— the BTK killer, and Ted Bundy, all had grown up in healthy households and had supportive families.

Another popular belief that surrounds the serial killers is that they are mostly white men. However, contrary to this widely accepted concept, serial killers could belong to any race. For example, Charles Ng, who killed numerous people in Northern California, was a native of Hong Kong. Similarly, Derrick Todd Lee, who was responsible for killing around 6 women in Louisiana, was an African-American. Coral Eugene Watts was also an African-American who murdered 5 people in Michigan and then fled to Texas in order to avoid detection. He was arrested, but only when he had killed another 12 people there.

Another way to identify the chances of someone turning into a serial killer is to scan their brains for anomalies. Many researchers believe that damage to the brain especially to the hypothalamus, the frontal lobe, and the limbic system can result in a person becoming extremely aggressive showing poor judgment and loss of control. The case of Henry Lucas proves this theory as he was reported to have severe brain damage in the areas mentioned. He was responsible for killing 11 people.

Further research on the topic such as conducted by the University of Wisconsin, Madison has revealed that brain damage of such individuals' results in a loss in connectivity between the ventromedial prefrontal cortex (vmPFC) and the amygdala. The relation between the damage to these regions of the brain and violence is because they are involved in the processing of the negative stimuli into negative responses and emotions. When the connectivity decreases between the two portions, people lose their ability to empathize and feel remorse for their bad actions.

While there have been reports of female serial killers, the chances of a female becoming a serial killer are almost negligible compared to that of men. There is a study that claims that 90% of the serial killers are male. The main idea that the male population is more inclined towards becoming serial killers, read the next chapter.

"We Serial killers are your sons, we are your husbands, we are everywhere, and there will be more of your Children dead tomorrow"

These are the words of Ted Bundy

Chapter 9

Serial Killing and Gender

Humans have curiosity embedded in their nature. Researchers like psychologist Marvin Zuckerman noted this morbid curiosity of human beings a long time ago. They acknowledge that there is something fascinating about terror and horror that simply catches our attention. This makes murder an extremely alluring business to all of us. Yet, what could be more attention grabbing than serial killing, which accounts for the increasing number of such cases.

A few years ago, only male serial killers were discussed and acknowledged and it is only recently that female serial killers have been taken into account as well. Even today, while everybody knows about Ted Bundy and Jeffrey Dahmer, not many are aware that Nannie Doss and Belle Gunness have committed crimes that were not less hideous either. Gunness was responsible for killing 25 people which included her own children and husbands, while Doss murdered about 11 people in the 20th century, which included her mother and grandson.

A number of researchers and psychologists who have studied the topic in detail support the theory that the act of serial killing is an exclusively male forte. The major names that backed this theory include the likes of Egger and Leyton. However, Hickey in the year 1991 discovered that women's representation in serial killing is equal to their involvement in another kind of killings in the United States. Yet, compared to men, women are still less likely to commit a serial killing and in most the cases where females are involved in a serial killing situation, they are accompanied with a male accomplice. Yet, there is no way to completely rule out the probability of a female becoming a serial murderer.

How does the MOD differ with women?

When it comes to studying female serial killers, not much research is available. However, the most important work on the subject comes from the famous Fresno State criminologist Eric Hickey. The author of the famous book of Serial Murderers and their Victims was successful in providing a profound insight on the topic with his 64 interviews with female serial killers in the United States. He was able to erect a disturbing image of female serial killers who shot, stabbed, and poisoned a number of men, other women, and children. His studies revealed an extremely crucial piece of information about female serial killers. We have studied them in detail and these are recorded in this chapter.

Most of the female serial killers, according to his studies, were white and commonly killed around 7 to 10 victims. Moreover, they were found to be more likely to murder their own family members than killing strangers. Also, the most common motive behind the murders was money even though these women belonged to the upper middle and upper classes.

In addition to this extensive study provided by Hickey, a number of studies with smaller samples have been conducted as well. For example, three people, Victoria Titterington, Amanda Farrell, and Robert Keppel, reviewed the newspaper reports for 10 American female serial killers in a 2011 study. Their findings concluded that female serial killers operate longer than a male serial killer does and 80% knew their victims. Another important finding on female serial killers came from Farrell, her colleagues, and Deborah Schurman-Kauflin. They interviewed around 8 female serial killers in 2000 and pointed out in their study nursing was a prevailing occupation among the female serial killers.

Studying Female Serial Killers

In order to further study the matter, sources such as Murderpedia.org were used. Also, in addition to identifying what makes female serial killers different from male serial killers, we were also interested in their psychology. This is a mass media approach and the results comply with the previous findings as well.

Following are the main points of the mass media research on the female serial killers:

• Financial Status: Most female serial killers belong to financially stable backgrounds and are not in want of money yet their biggest motive for killing was found to be money.

• Race and MO: 92% of the women knew their victims beforehand and almost all of them were white. Their most reliable and most commonly used method was poison.

• Education and Jobs: Most of the female serial killers that are reported and caught had earned college degrees. Many of them had a reliable job as well. Their field of work ranges from a prostitute to a religious teacher. However, 40% of these killers turned out to be from health related fields such as aides and nurses. Moreover, around 22% belonged to direct care giving roles such as babysitters or mothers.

• Marital Status: Most of the female serial killers were married at least at some point in their lives. Some of them were serial monogamists, being married from twice to as much as seven times. Most of these women were either average or above average in beauty and attractiveness and where the religion could be ascertained, all of the subjects turned out to be Christians.

• Strangers Versus Relatives: Around two-thirds of the female serial killers murdered people who were related to them. One-third of the studies group had killed their significant others and a surprising 44% had been guilty of murdering their own children. A little more than half of the studied female serial killers had targeted children while one-quarter had murdered the elderly or people who could not show much resistance.

An Evolutionary Perspective on Female Serial Killers

Considering the results of the detailed analysis of the female serial killers, we have found that there is a general consensus on the fact that money is almost always the driving force for the women to commit such felonies. Unlike men, they are not after sex. This general difference between the motives of the two sexes can account for a famous evolutionary psychological theory.

In 1972, Robert Trivers postulated that females possess a limited reproductive potential because of their fewer ova and therefore they have evolved to give more importance to securing resources. This could possibly mean looking for the best mate in the environment as well. Meanwhile, males have unlimited sperm and so they seek multiple opportunities to mate.

Having evolved differently does not make us serial killers though. The reasons for why someone turns towards such acts could be totally different, but the gender difference definitely plays an important role in determining the modus operandi and motives of the killer.

The other important point that can be deduced from the research is that male serial killers usually stalk, torture, and murder strangers, while female serial killers mostly kill their own relatives or people they know and are close to them. This makes the male serial killers the hunters and female serial killers the gatherers. Strangely that sounds a lot like the roles they had been playing since time immemorial.

While there is still no definite way to identify which young girl would grow up to become a serial killer, understanding the basic difference in the methods and motives male and female serial killers could definitely help with better profiling. For example, if a case of serial killings arises, you can look for certain things to at least identify the gender of the killer. This would narrow down your search to a great degree.

"I didn't want to hurt them, I only wanted to Kill them"

The words of David Berkowitz

"The Son of Sam"

Chapter 10

Conclusion

The topic of serial killing is vast and this book is like a small drop in the ocean. This is an attempt to spread awareness among the masses that are oblivious to the dangers of serial murders. With all the information provided in this book on serial killers and their never-ending desire to kill, we can draw a few interesting conclusions that will help us in the future.

First of all, serial killing is not a modern method of murder. It has been around since a long time ago, but was not properly acknowledged or reported. The first famous case was that of Jack, the Ripper. After that, there have been several cases of this form of killing.

Next, we have learned that serial killers are cold creatures with no remorse and guilt for their actions. A number of examples are cited in this book to shed light on the nature of these predators. However, the killers are in most cases are not crazy and are often fully aware of the consequences of their actions. Knowing their nature and personalities can help Law Enforcement with identifying and catching them. Even though there is no certain way to know who will become a serial killer in the future, are some signs that should be taken into consideration.

We have also discussed the root cause of the development of such diseased minds. The most popular argument concerning the topic is whether serial killers are psychopaths or sociopaths. While they show tendencies for both personality types, the votes for sociopathy are more than those for psychopathy. This makes it a problem of society and its permanent eradication requires us to make a few changes in the society turning it more flexible and tolerant. The most common factors resulting in the creation of such monsters include neglect and abuse in their childhood especially at the hands of their family, head injuries causing damage to their frontal lobe, social awkwardness, and an inability to fit in their surroundings.

Finally, we discussed the role of gender in serial killing. There are a lesser number of female serial killers than male serial killers and their motives differ as well. While women mostly kill for money, men are after sex. Also, women tend to kill the people they know while men murder strangers. This could have an evolutionary reason behind it.

In conclusion, we could say that while there is no definite way to identify a potential serial killer, we should look for the signs using the extensive research that has been conducted on the subject. I truly believe that serial Killers are not born into their behaviors, but are created whether be by personal emotional traumas or physical injuries. When completing my research it was clear to me from the information gathered, that the one thought, that was always constant with these predators, is their ideology that was "You will never know what lies behind my Eyes".

www.ingramcontent.com/pod-product-compliance
Lightning Source LLC
Chambersburg PA
CBHW050733030426
42336CB00012B/1544